To Sanjay
All the Best
"[illegible]"

STILL MOMENTS

STILL MOMENTS

A Story about Faded Dreams
and
Forbidden Pictures

ZIGHEN AYM

ZAWP / Permissions
PO Box 411
Mossville, IL 61552-0411

This is a work of non-fiction. Either the last or the full names of the people have been changed or omitted to protect their privacy. Those of the FBI agents have been omitted for obvious reasons.

Pictures by Zighen Aym

The cartoon, "Damned if you do, Damned if you don't," reprinted by kind permission of Khalil Bendib.

Publisher's Cataloging-In-Publication Data,
prepared by The Donohue Group, Inc.

Aym, Zighen.
Still moments : a story about faded dreams and forbidden pictures / Zighen Aym
—1st ed.

p. : ill. ; cm.
Includes bibliography.
ISBN: 0-9765998-0-5

1. Algerians—United States—Personal narratives. 2. Terrorism investigation—United States. 3. Racial profiling in law enforcement—United States. 4. Human rights—Algeria. 5. Photography—Political aspects—United States. I. Title.

E184.A55 A96 2005
973.93/092 LC Number 2005921997

For my mother, who used to say:
Eddem-ed taqejmuṛt, teṭṭfed taktabt
Take a stool and go read a book

For my wife and two children, for their support and patience.

For my friends who read my drafts, I remain in their debt forever. If readers happen to find errors and/or find the text too intense, I bear complete responsibility.

Dedicated to the hundreds of innocent people who were wrongly accused and subjected to abuse and deportation after the 9/11 events. Their personal stories might never be known.

Dedicated to the members of AWARE, the Anti-War Anti-Racism Effort of Urbana-Champaign, Illinois, whose members, even on cold and snowy days, came out on Prospect Avenue to protest the War on Iraq.

TABLE OF CONTENTS

PREFACE

by

Eric Sellin

Professor Emeritus, Tulane University

Zighen Aym's brief memoir is told with anger and humor. Thank God for the latter quality, for Aym's misadventures as a serious photographer taking pictures of railroad tracks and, of course, as an Algerian-American taking pictures in public in the post-9/11 United States, present a very disturbing scenario of ethnic profiling and a touch of paranoia on the part of the American authorities. The Patriot Act and the evergrowing intrusion of the Homeland Security team on individual liberties tend to rely on intimidation to achieve their goals... and these goals are not really crystal clear.

As a creative writer, I find the far-reaching actions of government—with regard to all of us Americans, native-born or naturalized—quite frightening. We are confronted with a growing blend of censorship and self-censorship of the kind usually found in countries which many of our immigrants have fled. René Steinke recently wrote in *The Literary Review*, which he edits: "In early March, the U.S. Treasury Department warned publishers that to edit any manuscript from Iran (or from any other nation with whom the United States has an embargo) would constitute 'trading with the enemy,' and those publishers who ignored the warning would face serious legal consequences. This, in effect, bans translations of texts from Iran, and by implication, from other countries such as Cuba, Libya, and North Korea" (TLR 47:3, Spring 2004, p. 3). We are, here, but a nuance away from banning creative "trade" with a nebulous group of people, starting with those who must be fingerprinted upon entering the United States.

Zighen Aym is doing himself proud as a naturalized American by telling his tragic-comic tale of his brush with the FBI. He is a fine photographer whose beautiful work has been published in a good many journals; and one need only look at the photographs published here—from that of a spider in its glistening web to that of telephone poles, a barn, and a bird in flight—to appreciate Aym's sensitive artistic eye.

In essence, one might declare that in the long run no harm was done, but who can estimate the emotional trauma to someone who thought to have found in the United States a haven from the terrors he had experienced in his previous homeland? In describing this harrowing episode, Aym shares with us his anxieties, frustrations, and bewilderment at being fingered as a suspicious character for innocently pursuing his hobby and for being, as he says, brown-skinned.

He has done us all a favor by courageously speaking out about his plight in this particular episode which is but a sample of the sort of singling out that certain ethnic groups are often subject to these days in the United States.

PROLOGUE

I must have become pregnant with this book soon after the FBI interrogated me in January 2003. At first, memories of the interrogation disappeared, probably drowned in a sea of denial; then bits of the questioning would sometimes surface only to be pushed down by an ever-growing pain. The pregnancy came to term the following April when my experience started to transform itself into sentences. As paragraphs continued to form and grow, so did a reluctance to share my personal feelings.

Although the writing process has been somewhat therapeutic, the recovery from the questioning has left me bitter and bewildered. Moreover, many issues remain unresolved. The first is the reversal of my emotions; my heart, once filled with dreams and hopes during my odyssey from Algeria to America, now overflows with fear and pain. The second is my inability to accept the fact that the unapologetic people who profiled me as a terrorist are getting away with it. The third is the idea that, after all things are considered, living in socialist Algeria under hardship, including standing in line for hours just to buy a bag of garbanzo beans and a few sticks of butter for my family, might have been more rewarding than coming to the US to earn a doctorate only to be suspected of terrorism later.

On the one hand, this blatant racial discrimination has shattered my optimism. On the other, it has opened my eyes and allowed me to see firsthand the sad reality of racial profiling and the beast that feeds on it.

During a recent summer visit to Algeria, I found myself unable to share my story with my 70-year-old parents. They would have never believed that US authorities suspected their highly educated son of terrorism.

"I knew it," my wife said after she finished reading my first draft.

"You knew what?" I asked.

"You said that the interview went fine," she explained, "but your story has just confirmed my worries that it was a terrible experience."

I felt my body tremble and needed to steel myself again.

"What do you want to do with the story?" my wife asked.

"I'll try to publish it. I might at least recoup the $268 the lawyer cost me to prove that I had nothing to do with terrorism," I answered jokingly.

"Maybe you'll be in bigger trouble after its publication," she said.

"Who knows?" I answered.

1

The Call

> Each one of us is guilty for the sole reason that we belong to a category, a race, a people. You fear that someone will attack you only because nobody has done it yet.
>
> **Mouloud Feraoun**
>
> *Journal 1954-1962: Reflections on the French-Algerian War*

January 22, 2003 would have been uneventful enough to be forgotten if it were not for the phone that rang at about 5:30 p.m. I had just gotten home from work. My two children, sitting in the dining room, were completing their homework, and my wife was still at work. I was explaining an eighth grade algebra problem to my oldest child when that call came. I went to the kitchen, picked up the cordless handset, and heard a stranger say, "This is Agent Robert H. from the FBI office in Normal. We got a report from the state police that you were taking pictures of trains, and I would like to talk to you. I called you last week and left a message…"

The FBI? I vaguely remembered an unclear phone message on our old answering machine a few days earlier. However, I usually do not pay attention to messages unless I recognize the voice. I had thought that the message was from a telemarketer or service provider looking for prospective clients, so I had erased it.

After I confirmed that yes, an Illinois State trooper had stopped me almost three months earlier, Agent Robert continued:

"In these times of terrorism, I would like to follow up on the report and talk to you. Could I meet you at your house to ask you a few questions about your love of trains?"

His words jolted me. The FBI's interest in me was disturbing. In a state of denial, refusing to have my life connected to a federal police agency, I hoped to hear a friend's voice burst into laughter, indicating it was a prank call. But there would be no friend's voice because the one friend I had told about my encounter with the state trooper was a woman.

My mind scrambled for words. To refuse his request for questioning and any connection with him, I managed to say:

"I don't love trains."

When it dawned on me that this call really was from the FBI, I chose to continue the conversation in our basement. I did not want my children to overhear anything that might upset them. They usually ask "Who was it?" and "What did he or she want?" after a phone call. I did not want to have to lie, nor did I want them to know that it was the FBI because they would worry about it.

"I prefer not in my house, but maybe in your office?" I suggested as I attempted to remember what my rights, if any, were. I was not sure if I could refuse to meet with him, but I knew with some certainty that I could refuse to meet him at our home.

The agent turned down my offer and reiterated his preference to meet at our home, which, in turn, I refused. The last thing I wanted was a couple of well-dressed FBI agents knocking at our door. Their visit would probably reinforce any suspicion my neighbors might already have about my family and me. Except for the mess of books, articles and pictures in my office, I had nothing to hide. The intrusion into my private life would be a humiliating experience.

To cut short our disagreement on the venue for our meeting, I decided to stall and asked:

"May I have your name and phone number and let you know after I talk to my lawyer?"

After I got his contact information and quietly but quickly hung up the phone, I felt as if time had stopped, and I experienced my second still moment right there. Then a rush of thoughts stormed my mind, yet none justified the FBI phone call. Bizarre as it seemed then, I was torn between worry and laughter. I was confused and, for the first time, unable to think clearly. It was as if I had come to a crossroads without any road signs. On the one hand, I worried about being arrested and unjustly detained. On the other, I felt like bursting into laughter, as the FBI's suspicion of me seemed very ludicrous. It was very hard to accept the change from my role as a silent spectator to the events that followed the 9/11 attacks to the role of a suspected terrorist. I remained in the basement as I struggled to find a logical explanation for this suspicion.

The FBI's interest in me was a mix of irony and surprise. The first was that I was suspected of being a terrorist here in America after I fled Algeria twelve years earlier to escape its repressive regime and its terrorism. The second was that I thought the FBI went after criminals instead of people photographing old barns, spiders, and railroad tracks.

But history was only repeating itself; for this was not the first time I had attracted the attention of law enforcement authorities for taking pictures, except that the three previous times had occurred in Algeria. Whether I took a picture of ships in a harbor, graffiti on a wall near a police station, or a sand dune near an oil-pumping station in the desert, I found myself having to prove that photography was a hobby and that I was not spying for a foreign agency or government. However, this time, something was definitely different. As I was to find out later, my skin color made my taking pictures appear suspicious.

Confused and tired, I sat on a chair. I wanted to focus more intently on what had just happened. Yet, I found myself standing up a second later as if my body was telling me to do something. I did not know what I could do: I had no reason to run away, because I had neither done anything wrong nor broken any law.

I sat down again and closed my eyes. Then for the first time, I heard a strange voice:

"Have you been asleep? I've been trying to talk to you."

I dismissed the voice and said to myself:

"Calm down and think logically now."

"You thought you were safe here in America," the voice continued.

Until then, my conscience had consisted of only one voice – the true voice of my thoughts and mind, a familiar one that I had grown up with, the one that has been guiding my life for as long as I could remember. Although the new voice sounded as if it belonged to someone else, it, too, was in my head. It said, "What if you get arrested and detained without access to a lawyer, your family, and the outside world? What if your detention turns into a physical disappearance?" The FBI was a powerful organization, and such things have happened to others. In this new and post 9/11 world, the FBI had the power to arrest me while it sought potential evidence of terrorist activities. These were the fears, scary but realistic, that the voice kept feeding me.

Until that time, I did not remember ever having heard the voice speak to me. Besides, if I had heard it, I had not paid attention to it because I had refused to think of myself as a potential victim in America. I had not become a disillusioned new immigrant. After all, I had played by the rules of society. Therefore I found it more pleasing to focus on positive aspects of life in my adopted country. Nevertheless, it now seemed as if I had only sidestepped the issue of racial and ethnic discrimination, one of the ugly and unpleasant facts of life. The post 9/11 events, my American friends' concerns about our safety, my encounter with the state trooper, and now the call from the FBI, formed a pattern that I needed to heed and to take into account.

The new voice communicated thoughts that I could not easily dismiss, because ignoring them could be detrimental. Yet, I was reluctant to let fear and bitterness into my mind.

The FBI's suspicion seemed crazy and surreal. Yet, it was real and scary indeed, and I needed to consider its consequences fully. Of course, I wanted to shut out the new voice and to forget the call. I needed a temporary relief and a warmer refuge for my confused mind. My thoughts left our basement in Central Illinois and sought moments of hope in my past. Needing emotional balance and strength, I searched my memories and stumbled upon one that was almost a quarter of a century old.

At that time, I was a twenty-three-year-old undergraduate student at Tulane University in New Orleans. Early one morning, I arrived at the help desk of the Computing Services when my supervisor walked towards me, his right hand extended for a handshake:

"Good job," Irving said, smiling and firmly shaking my hand.

Surprised, I said, "Thank you. But for what?"

"For helping us release the hostages," he said. It was January 26, 1981, one day after Algeria had helped negotiate the release of the American hostages from Iran.

"But I did not do anything to release them," I said with a measure of modesty.

"Well, Zighen, I'd like to thank Algeria for helping us free our people, but since you are the only Algerian I know, I have no one else to thank but you," he said.

The "times of terrorism," the FBI agent mentioned during the phone call, referred, of course, to the times after the tragic events of 9/11. The scenes of the airplanes ripping through the towers and the ensuing destruction had stunned me. The TV images were unbelievable, beyond comprehension. When I first saw them in the workplace cafeteria, tears had filled my eyes. Just like in Algeria, civilians in America had fallen victim to indiscriminate violence.

Unfortunately, in the aftermath of 9/11, several acts of violence were committed in America against innocent people with Middle Eastern, North African, and East Asian appearances. Yet many Americans showed their solidarity with innocent people from these regions and stood up to protect them. In Central Illinois, members of Normal's New Covenant Community Church kept watch in the lobby of the Bloomington-Normal Islamic Center during a prayer service. American friends, Annette and Maurer in Louisiana, Mary Ann in North Carolina, and Katherine in Virginia contacted us, inquired about our safety, and advised us to be careful. Their hospitality, continued friendship, and concerns brought a ray of hope to our lives after 9/11. With some apprehension, my family and I attempted to carry on with our lives.

The first Friday after the 9/11 attacks, as an American colleague and I left a local restaurant, he offered to walk me to my car. His offer surprised me when I realized that he was concerned for my safety and not merely being gallant. When I indicated that I felt safe because I had done nothing wrong, he said, "Zighen, there are people out there, right now, who do not care a bit about your innocence."

"How could America allow this?" I inquired for I considered my new home as the land of justice for all and where one is innocent until proven guilty.

After a pause, Eric said, "All I can say is do not go to unfamiliar places where people don't know you."

The idea that I might become a target had never crossed my mind. It was an unpleasant matter that lacked justification and was unacceptable; nothing in my life had prepared me for it. I grew up in North Africa, a region successively invaded by the Phoenicians, Romans, Vandals, Byzantines, Arabs, Turks, Spaniards, and the French, where people's skin, hair, and eye colors are very diverse but hardly a racial and political issue.

When I came to America in 1977, I found out just how much skin color separated people. As a newcomer, I did not know to which group I belonged. Because my tan color appeared to be a middle ground between black and white, I thought I was shielded from this issue. However, deep in me, I knew that associating a skin color with actions was preposterous. Both brain and skin, two distinct organs, could not share the same function in a human body. And I continued to believe that most people did not judge others by their skin color and that the official claims of justice, equality and opportunity for everyone were genuine.

Lingering in my mind, my friends' concerns started to weigh in, and I could no longer censor the thought of becoming a target.

"What happened to the feeling of security you have been accustomed to since your arrival in the US?" the voice asked, as if in a challenge.

"The question is whether that feeling might have simply been a fruit of my imagination," I thought.

Thereafter, while shopping in stores or walking in streets or parks, I found myself scrutinizing and analyzing the way people looked at me, wondering if their greetings were sincere and whether they noticed my complexion. I once went as far as imagining them attacking me as I walked by them. Another time, I even refrained from greeting people because I was afraid to attract the attention of a vengeful person.

The new circumstances required a new interpretation of things. Did I misread the thoughts of the beautiful and elegant women surreptitiously staring at me in stores before 9/11? My innocent yet probably naïve guess had been that they were fantasizing about the tall, tanned man that I was. Some would lower their eyes as if they had been caught doing something they should not have been doing. Others would attempt to get hold of themselves and arrange a smile with their red-painted lips. Could I have been that wrong? Could their eyes have instead seen a terrorist in me? What a change of perspective!

Across the nation, the FBI began to arrest hundreds of people, and indiscriminate and violent attacks on people from North Africa, the Middle East, and Eastern Asia continued to be reported. Because my troubles could come either from people bent on revenge or from those who are supposed to protect me, I felt doubly targeted. As I continued to worry, my belief in America as a safe heaven started to fade, my optimistic outlook on life began to blur, and my dream of a glowing future in my new country dimmed. My journey from North Africa to North America seemed somehow less exciting, and a strange feeling of fear, an inch below panic, started to creep into my mind.

The FBI's suspicion of me—as was later confirmed—lay not in anything I had done but in the color of my skin. When I came back to America in 1990, I never thought that one day I would become a target of racism. That was why I could not think of myself as one. Instead, the FBI's interest in me stimulated my curiosity in the matter. In addition, I found in the interest an opportunity to resist according to my principles: to act and to attempt to change things. By refusing the FBI agent's terms—to meet him at our home—I thought I was already making myself accountable to these principles. The FBI might have the power and the upper hand, but I was not going to let myself become a victim of their authority.

That is when another interpretation of their interest in me suddenly crossed my mind. Their need to meet me amounted to a definite weakness on their side. They wanted something they thought I had. Somehow, I had power too.

2

Spiders and Railroad Tracks

> When you see an injustice being committed, try to stop it. If you can't, then protest loudly against it. If you can't do even that, at least condemn it in your heart.
>
> **Prophet Muhammed**

I dreamt of America when I was in North Africa in the early 1990's. "You will see. Our life in America will be so different from here," I remember telling my wife as we stood on the balcony of her parents' home in Notre Dame d'Afrique, a hilltop suburb of Algiers overlooking the coast of the Mediterranean Sea. "Laws protect people and dreams come true," I had explained to her.

In leaving Algeria and its violent political situation, my wife and I wanted to shield ourselves from the violence, repression, and injustice that had been plaguing Algeria for the last fifteen years.

In America, we wished to find freedom, tranquility, and plenty of opportunities to pursue our dreams. As we headed to New Orleans, where I had been accepted into the Ph.D. program at Tulane University, it was like coming back to my second home. Eight years earlier, I had lived in the fabled southern city as an undergraduate student.

Upon our arrival I reconnected with old friends, and my wife and I started new friendships among the university's cosmopolitan community. We both looked forward to our new life with hope and excitement.

Unfortunately, terrible news from Algeria was only a phone call away. In May 1997, we learned that my wife's 19-year-old sister was killed along with five of her class-mates when a bomb exploded near the entrance of her high school in downtown Algiers. As a senior, she had already made plans to attend college in the fall. Another time, the news was that my wife's uncle, a film producer, had been stabbed several times in front of his house, but luckily he survived the attack.

After I received my Ph.D. in 1998, my family and I moved from the Crescent City to Central Illinois where life became mundane, consisting of only work and everyday chores. However, my exploration of scenic views of flat lands and cornfields was going to alter all that.

One early day in October 2002, I drove to work along Route 66, the fabled, two-lane road and discovered histori-cal remnants of a unique place in American culture. Going northbound past the little town of Towanda, I saw the sun-rise to my right. Its bright rays exposed the gray and black shapes of distant houses, farms, barns, and trees, all the way to the horizon. Closer to the road, the sunlight revealed the beautiful form of spider webs woven and moored to the tall grasses. Laden with small droplets of dew that reflected the sunlight, the web strings shone with hundreds of tiny lights.

The Saturday after, I woke up before sunrise to return to the city of spiders, where I found the residents of the shining webs still asleep in the post-dawn light. The silky strands of each web were like the concentric paths of planets around the spider in the center. The strands of some webs were broken, the result of a heavy accumulation of dew or the struggle with a difficult prey the day before. Soon the sun peered slowly over the horizon and its rays bathed the spiders. Their motionless bodies sparkled with dewdrops just like the strands of their webs. Then each arachnid stretched its legs just like a baby waking up after a good night's sleep, a fascinating display of one of life's miracles. After a few moments, they set out to complete the first of their daily chores: checking the condition of their webs and moving meticulously from one node to another. Not until each spider had repaired its webs completely did it rest. Sensing my footsteps, one spider dropped to the ground on a new silk strand and hid under the small grass.

The following Monday, despite the sun's presence, the dozens of webs failed to shine on the side of Route 66 as I drove to work. The grasses had been mowed, probably to prevent fires. I was sad to see the spider neighborhood destroyed and hoped that the little creatures, warned by the noise of the engine, had had time to drop and hide in the lower uncut grass.

Late on the afternoon of October 18, 2002, I was driving home from work on Route 66 when two barns, one old and one new, attracted my attention. They sat there in a yellow-brown sea of recently cut corn stalks, like two friends engaged in a conversation about old times, as pigeons swooped in from the clear blue sky to rest on their roofs. The scenery moved me so much that I stopped my car to take a few distant pictures and then walked towards them for close-up shots. My eye then traveled across the road to where a row of five corn elevators stood next to the rail tracks. I crossed the road and came upon the two rails, their flat surfaces reflecting sunlight and shining like two silver lines drawn into the horizon. To their right, a seemingly infinite series of old telephone poles bordered the tracks. Many were still standing straight with their green and transparent glass petticoat insulators on them; others were leaning with their broken wires falling to the ground; still others lay on the ground.

The scene of the converging rail tracks and obsolete telephone poles was a harmonious display of increasing distance and decreasing height and span; a natural 3-D visual agreement. About 30 feet to my right was Route 66, where a few trucks and cars still ventured as the day was ending. I bent my knees, lowered my body, and took a few shots of the rail tracks. I continued to look through the camera viewfinder to compose the next picture when I noticed a northbound car with its headlights turned on. A careful look indicated the car belonged to the Illinois State Police. I quickly snapped a picture.

As I lifted my head, I wondered if the state trooper came to question me. I watched as the police car slowed down and turned at the road where I had parked my car. Then I remembered the new directives about homeland security that had asked ordinary citizens to be on the lookout for potential perpetrators of acts of terrorism. Yes, I was now sure of the purpose of the police dispatch. I realized that I had never seen other people take scenic pictures on Route 66, and that a person with my TNT profile must have seemed even more unusual to drivers and passengers on Route 66. (Oops, I forgot to explain TNT. No, it is not the acronym for Trinitrotoluene, an explosive chemical compound. It means Tall and Naturally Tanned.) An hour had probably already passed since I had stopped to take pictures of the barns, certainly enough time for an overzealous citizen traveling on Route 66 to report me and for a state trooper to be dispatched. This sudden realization froze time for me. It was my first still moment.

"Well, Zighen, you are going to be checked out right here, right now," I teased myself in order to remain calm. It was definitely not the time to lose control of myself.

After the trooper's car came to a halt just past mine, a clean-shaven officer in full khaki gear got out, adjusted his circular state trooper's hat, and walked towards me. I stood up, making sure not to point my camera at him; I did not want him to mistake it for a gun for I had read on numerous occasions about police officers accidentally shooting unarmed citizens who held objects in their hands. An imagined headline, "Suspect Shot While Taking Pictures of Railway Tracks," in Bloomington's *The Pantagraph* would have certainly convinced readers of my culpability.

I waited—I was not afraid, but I realized that I was unfortunately alone facing an armed man. His dispatch to investigate the photographer on Route 66 showed hints of ethnic profiling in the horizon. At that moment, I remembered Bruce Springsteen's song "American Skin" in which a black mother tries to get her young son to make her a promise: to understand the rules, be polite, never run, and keep his hands in sight.

"What are we doing here?" the trooper asked with professional courtesy.

I was relieved to hear a question. A few hours before dark, he had not mistaken the camera in my hand for a gun. However, his use of the "we" as the sentence subject puzzled me.

"Taking pictures," I answered, thinking it should have been obvious.

"For what?" he continued.

"My hobby," I replied as I attempted to be both truthful and succinct.

I considered quoting Thomas Jefferson's preamble to the American Constitution, which enshrined "life, liberty, and pursuit of happiness;" because photography, a hobby I had picked up almost a quarter of a century earlier, has allowed me to focus on the beauty of nature, record life, and enrich my mind.

"Where are you from?" he continued.

The question, which amounted to "you don't belong here" hit me like a rock although he asked it in the same courteous tone he had used for the first two questions.

"Here," I answered seriously. My home was only about 30 miles away.

"Where is here?" he pressured.

I wondered whether the trooper thought I was trying to be smart.

"Bloomington," I answered.

"Where do you work?" he asked.

I gave him the name of my employer and showed him my employee badge.

"Can I see your driver's license?" he asked.

I took it out from my wallet and handed it to him.

"Keep doing your work," he said. "I found it odd to see your car parked next to the rail tracks. I stopped to make sure everything was all right."

I remained silent.

He walked back to his car to call in my information and check my records. I felt confident, for I do not have any police record. I considered myself a typical law-abiding citizen.

I attempted to resume taking pictures, but the moment had definitely passed. The question "Where are you from?" had discomfited me; the state trooper's presence intimidated me; I had an unusual feeling of powerlessness. Yet, I remained calm and walked slowly back to my car. I glanced at the officer in his car just before I got into mine. He was talking on his radio and looking at the back of my car, probably calling in my license plate number.

3

Déjà Vu

There may be times when we are powerless to prevent injustice, but there must never be a time when we fail to protest.

Elie Wiesel

As I waited patiently inside my car for the state trooper to run a police check on me, I remembered another time when photography precipitated an encounter with a police authority. In 1986, a friend and I were visiting the Mediterranean coastal city of Bejaia, located 150 miles east of Algiers, Algeria. We were at Guidon Place, a tourist area overlooking the industrial port and the adjacent bay. My friend had gone to buy a newspaper, and while I waited for him, I lifted my camera and started to look through the viewfinder, aiming at cargo ships being loaded and unloaded on the wharf down below. The sea was calm, but the sky was laden with heavy clouds, an omen of coming rain. Suddenly, I felt a light tap on my shoulder. When I turned around, I found myself facing a policeman who asked me to refrain from taking pictures.

"But this is only the port…" I objected. It was not a military compound, and I was in a tourist area.

"Yes, but behind you is a bank," he said as he pointed to the offices of the National Bank of Algeria.

"I did not know that," I explained.

"You don't need to know that. I know it," he added.

"Yes, but I have pointed my camera towards the ships, and the bank is behind me," I said.

"The risk is that your camera could be a spy camera with a special device to take pictures at 180 degrees," he said unfaltering.

"Okay," I answered, realizing the impossibility to win the argument with a government agent.

The policeman walked away, and my friend returned and inquired:

"What did the policeman want?"

"He is crazy," I replied as I rotated my right index finger around my right temple and recounted the incident.

We were about to stroll along when a hand suddenly grabbed my arm. It was the same policeman. This time he had a much less pleasant expression on his face.

"You told your friend I was out of my mind," he shouted, "I am taking you to the station."

Little did I know that, although he had walked away, he had kept watching me to see whether I would keep taking pictures. He had therefore seen me make the crazy sign with my hand and understood that I had referred to him.

He asked for my national identity card and instructed me to follow him to the police station. There he inquired about my date of birth, place of birth, place of work, and title. He said that he considered my offensive hand sign to be an insult to the Algerian nation and added that all Algerians, government officials and citizens, too, should be concerned with Algeria's security. Then he started proudly and flawlessly to recite the government line on the impending foreign threat to Algeria. It was an accurate repetition of the propaganda hammered in by the official and mainstream media.

"Algeria is a jewel. We, the people, can jeopardize it if we do not take precautions. We have to be careful and protect our independence from foreign powers, especially the imperialists and the old colonists," he proudly proclaimed.

At the time, Algeria, which had gained independence from France in 1962 after a seven-year bloody revolution, was run by the FLN (the French acronym for the National Liberation Front). Three years later, Algeria started an ambitious and progressive socialist program: to industrialize the country and to educate the Algerian population, which had mostly remained poor and uneducated during the 132-year-long French occupation. As reported in Mouloud Fearoun's *The Poor Man's Son*, the illiteracy rate was as high as 86 percent among men and 95 percent among women in 1954 on the eve of the war for independence.

Thanks to Algeria's education program, thousands of men and women soon attended the newly constructed schools, colleges, and universities while the government offered scholarships to thousands of students to go overseas to gain expertise in science and technology. That is how I, the son of an illiterate Berber woman and a poor Berber peasant with only an elementary education from the Djurdjura Mountains, had been awarded a scholarship to study in America in 1977 and ultimately became an engineer.

At the station, the policeman had the authority, and I, the citizen, had to obey. To him, when Authority talked, the citizen had to listen and believe. And to the Authority, what is acceptable is when a citizen is docile or pretends to believe. I therefore listened attentively to the policeman and kept nodding, pretending to accept his arguments, but unfortunately validating his belief in his line of duty.

When I was finally allowed to speak, I explained that I had returned from America with a degree in engineering to work on the maintenance of oil-pumping equipment in the Sahara, thus participating in the building of socialist Algeria. Convinced, he let me go after an hour. I never heard from the Algerian police about that incident again. I could not help but wonder if the policeman was not busy that day and simply wanted to justify his salary and to show evidence of work to the police chief.

4

Voting for God

Silence is death
And if you speak, you die
If you are silent, you die
So speak and die

Tahar Djaout

Simultaneously ruling and embodying the state, Algeria's FLN party reached a level of a complete hegemony. It controlled every aspect of Algerian life, including culture, media, industry, agriculture, religion, trade unions, women and youth organizations, sports, and education. In the process, it saw the rise to power of corrupt and self-serving politicians, who took every opportunity to control people with the propaganda that kept them in power.

Although they still called their system socialism, it was more like state capitalism, for they controlled the country's wealth and resources. At that time, the billboard slogans read: "The revolution by the people for the people," "Socialism is our ideal," "Socialism is the abolition of men's exploitation of one by another," "Algeria is the land of socialism," and "Socialism means the well being of the people." Despite expressing the ideals of socialism, they were a tool for FLN party members to sneak into power and built personal fortunes.

The politicians went so far as to hold conferences to convince Algerians that their political system of governance was compatible with Islam, the country's state religion. And, of course, the Algerian mainstream media, under FLN control, uttered no criticism, and all non-FLN political activities were forbidden. As required by Article 120 of the FLN Statutes, even job promotions in state-owned companies required a membership in the FLN party. To criticize or to challenge the President or the FLN policies was considered counterrevolutionary and unpatriotic. To travel outside Algeria for a vacation or a family visit, one required both a passport and a special certificate of leave.

In the 1980s, despite its high oil and gas revenues, Algeria's economy deteriorated, evidenced by a shortage of housing, jobs, and opportunities. Food shortages resulted in long lines at state-run stores.

I remember one incident in 1986 when I strolled into a *Souk El-Fellah* (Farmer's Market in Arabic), a state-run shopping center mostly known for its dust-covered and empty shelves, near my hometown. A shipment of garbanzo beans and butter had arrived and was being sold. I felt lucky and even luckier when I counted the number of people in line and realized that I would probably be sold both chickpeas and butter. When I came out of the store loaded with ten pounds of garbanzo beans in one hand and four pounds of butter in the other, it was as if I had struck the lottery.

Heading home, I experienced a growing exhilaration, which reached a climax when I proudly displayed my groceries as trophies and told my mother: "Look what I got today!" However, my excitement was short-lived. My provisions started to look like the conditional stimulus in a Pavlovian experiment conducted by the Algerian government . The controlled shortage of provisions in Algeria was the government's tool of manipulation. It had lowered my expectations. In America and many other parts of the world, I knew that garbanzo beans and butter were available at any time of the day or night.

As years went by, the Algerian political system showed further signs of failure. The economy worsened, affecting every aspect of citizens' lives. Major riots erupted in Algiers in October 1988. Violence and death helped erase socialist propaganda from state-run media, and removed it from the leaders' rhetoric too. Blaming the bad economy on socialism, government officials began to praise capitalism and to push for reforms towards a market economy while they remained in power. By then, such an economy was clearly beneficial to them, for they had personally acquired much of the country's wealth. That was when the term "the political and financial Mafia," was coined to refer to the government and became a household expression in Algeria.

What had been impossible during Algeria's 26 years of independence became a surprising reality almost overnight when the government allowed other political parties to form. The ensuing political facade, painted and presented as a democratic overture, created not just two or three additional political parties but close to sixty. The government went as far as allowing the creation of an unconstitutional Islamic party, the FIS (a French acronym for Islamic Salvation Front). One of its leaders, Abassi Madani, a former FLN party member, advocated a return to an Islamic state based on the *sharia*, the religious laws, signaling a theocratic regime that would be even more repressive than the present one if it ever came to power. A campaign slogan "Vote for No. 6, Vote for God" on a banner in the city of Draa-Ben-Khedda during the 1990 municipal elections was a clear signal of religion getting into politics. The divine presence in political campaigns was no laughing matter. Dissent against a political program suggested by "God" would probably result in death if one did not repent, as the FIS leaders suggested. Who would dare object to a party that shrouds itself with divinity and claims to hold both moral and religious values?

Although fundamentalism did not show its claws until 1990, field preparations had started in the early 1970s with the state-funded promotional "campaign" of religious schooling and customs. Could the Algerian political and financial Mafia have prepared the political fields 20 years earlier? I remember driving in downtown Algiers in the summer of 1977 and being surprised by the huge crowds coming out of mosques after the evening prayers. A new brand of religious indoctrination had started to take hold.

The political power struggle continued between the military government and the fundamentalist militants. Invigorated by their participation in the war in Afghanistan against the Russians, armed militants held, upon their return, a victory parade with full army fatigues in downtown Algiers. Soon, an armed conflict pitted the fundamentalists against the government. In 1992, the military regime banned the FIS and forced the president to resign.

As the armed fundamentalist groups increased their attacks, the government passed a law that banned hunting guns and confiscated them from ordinary citizens. The government's premise was to stop the hunting guns from falling in the hands of terrorists. However, that also meant that during attacks, villagers and peasants were defenseless. As a result, civilians, caught in the middle, became sitting ducks: more than 200,000 Algerians and more than 100 foreigners have been murdered since 1990 by either the government or the armed fundamentalist groups. To explain this failure to protect the citizens, a former interior minister said that he could not possibly protect all Algerians for that would require a policeman for every citizen.

The violence that targeted civilians from all segments of Algerian society escalated: Murders took place in broad daylight, car and bus bombs exploded in crowded streets, and Algeria started on a spiraling journey of unspeakable atrocities. Decapitated heads were left on fence posts as gory warnings or trophies.

The first journalist to be killed was Tahar Djaout, a published Berber poet and writer. On what appeared to be a sham evening news on June 1, 1993, the Algerian police presented a 28-year-old man who confessed to the May 26 shooting of Djaout. He indicated that a *fatwa* (religious ruling) had been decreed against the journalist and noted that Tahar Djaout had a mighty pen and was a communist, a farfetched accusation but a fundamentalist's favorite one. Djaout's pen was indeed mighty: He owned a weekly newspaper *Ruptures* and published editorials that regularly criticized both the government and the fundamentalists for what they really were. Two of his books, *The Last Summer of Reason*, a posthumous work, and *The Watchers,* were recently published in the U.S. and were well received by the American readers and reviewers alike.

Prophetically, Djaout spoke out about speaking out, and he died on June 2 after lying for a week in a coma. Because he was a staunch critic of both the fundamentalist groups and the military government, either one or both could have been behind his assassination. More than 60 other journalists were murdered after him. Not surprisingly, many, like Djaout, were staunch critics of both the Algerian military government and the fundamentalist groups. The continued violence forced the remaining journalists and other intellectuals to go into either hiding or exile. As many as 400,000 Algerian intellectuals have reportedly left the country.

However, journalists, poets, artists, singers, critics of the government, and intellectuals in general were not the only targets of the violence. Entire families and sometimes villages were massacred, schools and factories burned, and people kidnapped, many never to be seen again.

On September 22, 1997, in the village of Bentalha, a distant suburb of Algiers, an army patrol stopped at a local café and warned a group of domino players: “You do not know what is in store for you tonight. It is going to be nasty for you.” By sunrise, more than 400 people lay dead after more than a hundred armed men burst into the village, shut down power, and slaughtered the inhabitants over a six-hour period. That night and despite the villagers' cries, the military personnel in the adjacent army barracks failed to intervene for they had received orders not to leave their compound.

That same month, the government negotiated a full amnesty with the leaders of the AIS (a French acronym for the Islamic Salvation Army), an organization of 6,000 terrorists and the armed wing of the FIS. Some of the them have since established businesses with the laundered money they amassed during their terrorist “careers;” others joined the Algerian military, and still others have re-enlisted in other armed groups. One of them is the GIA (a French acronym for Armed Islamic Group), a group that refused to negotiate with the government. This group has been reportedly infiltrated by Algerian security services. Some even say that it was created by the Algerian government. Two former Algerian military officers published detailed accounts about the infiltration and creation of the GIA by Algerian security services. Observers have indicated that the GIA's refusal of the amnesty gave the government reasons to maintain the state of siege, justifying and legitimizing the extra-judicial actions and keeping the people in a state of fear.

In 2003, the FLN successfully returned to power after 20 years of covert political operations and ten of thousands of Algerians dead. Today many observers argue that the Algerian political and financial Mafia planned the 1988 riots to convince the people that the new political era had begun. As for the FIS leader, Abassi Madani, the Algerian government allowed him to leave Algeria in 2004 for supposed health reasons. He now lives comfortably in Saudi Arabia, the same country that gave asylum to Idi Amin Dada, the notorious former president of Uganda who is known for his brutal and despotic rule in the 1970s.

More than fifteen years after the 1990 political overture, violence still plagues Algeria, and civilians meet their deaths at fake roadblocks and during night attacks. The country is officially still under a state of siege, which the government officials justify. They claim they need to fight terrorism, but they use this excuse to tighten their hold on power.

The word "socialism," now a taboo word, has completely disappeared from the Algerian political scene and is no longer extolled by government officials and media. They used socialism as their Trojan horse to sneak into positions of power and then hold on to them. Ironically, one of its staunchest promoters, Abdelaziz Bouteflika, Algeria's current president and foreign minister from 1966 to 1978, now advocates an outright liberal economy.

In a 2004 book titled "Bouteflika: An Algerian Fraud," a detailed investigation revealed a highly unflattering look at President Bouteflika and his political career. The author, Mohamed Benchicou, the publisher of the French-language daily *Le Matin* in Algeria, indicated that as a foreign minister Bouteflika instructed Algerian embassies and consulates to deposit their unspent budgets into private bank accounts in Switzerland. Although in 1979 the Algerian Audit Office charged him with misappropriating public money, Bouteflika sent a check that covered only a portion of the stolen money, drawn from a Geneva-based Swiss bank.

Unfortunately, at the time of this writing, Benchicou is serving a two-year sentence on charges that he violated Algeria's currency exchange laws. Many observers viewed the sentence as a retaliation for Benchicou's publication of his book about Bouteflika and for *Le Matin's* allegation that Interior Minister Yazid Zerhouni, a former Algerian Ambassador to the US from 1987-1992, had tortured detainees while he was a military security commander in the 1970s .

5

A *Faux Pas*

> If you stand up and are counted, you may get yourself knocked down. But remember this: A man flattened by an opponent can get up again. A man flattened by conformity stays down for good.
>
> **Watson, J. Thomas, Jr.**
> (1914 - 1993)

The noise of a passing truck brought me back to my car parked near Route 66. The trooper was still in his car too. The moment seemed historical, and I wanted to remember the exact words of the state trooper. I grabbed a pen and on the back of an envelope jotted down the trooper's words, "I found it odd to see your car parked next to the rail tracks. I stopped to make sure everything was all right." When I finished, I lifted my head only to see the trooper standing next to the car door.

"Oh, no!" I thought, "Did he read my notes? What next?"

He repeated his reason for investigating me and returned my ID. After he said I was free to go, I started my car, and at the same time I heaved a sigh of relief. I drove home, not sure what to make of my encounter with the trooper, except that, exactly a week later, the FBI issued a chillingly specific warning about imminent attacks on Amtrak trains. It indicated that attacks could take the form of exploding a bomb inside a train, demolishing a rail bridge, or derailing a train by damaging a rail bed. I was certain that the Illinois state troopers and other law enforcement agents had learned about the warnings before the public announcement. I thought that a request to follow up on my taking pictures must be already on its way.

Time passed and the holiday seasons came and went. I forgot all about the incident, but the law enforcement agencies had not, as I was to learn later.

"I have a surprise for you," I shouted to my wife from the basement when she got home on the day the FBI called.

"You lost your job?" she said, leaning on the basement staircase banister. At that time, my employer was in the process of streamlining its workforce.

"No, the FBI wants to interview me. They received a report about my taking pictures of railroad tracks three months ago," I said with a smile.

"The real FBI?" she inquired.

"The one and only," I confirmed. Her face became pale. To show her that she should not worry, I burst out in laughter.

"You think this is a joke!" she said, shocked to see me take such a matter lightheartedly.

"Not really, but I find it kind of amusing," I said.

The alternative, to fear the FBI and to imagine myself shackled and locked up in a federal prison, was too traumatic, unpleasant, and detrimental to my emotional health. But my wife, who is much more suspicious of law enforcement agencies, saw the sudden arbitrary change in policies towards people from North Africa, the Middle East, and East Asia as a threat. She believed their policies were nothing more than knee-jerk reactions that served more to avoid citizens' questions about the government's failure to protect the country from the 9/11 attacks.

To summarize the federal government's stance after 9/11, my wife had said:

"Look, Americans, some beasts are in jail. Some are on the run. Others are dead. You, the people, can now feel safe. We are protecting you,"

"When forces of authority, like those of nature, go into action, disasters and death follow, and only the poor and powerless people like us pay the price," she had added.

That rang true because, just after 9/11, the White House secretly ordered that law enforcement agencies allow 140 wealthy Saudis to be flown out of the US when all commercial and private flights were grounded. In addition, Muslim tyrants, presented as presidents and kings of North African or Middle Eastern countries, were officially hosted at the White House. Other Muslim princes and officials are regular and unofficial guests at the White House. One much richer Muslim king was hosted by his Christian friend at a ranch in Crawford, Texas. By contrast, poor and innocent, brown-skinned Muslim people like me, who could not afford to pack and go, were offered an unwanted, negative VIP service in the form of interrogations by the FBI or indiscriminate violence by poor and afraid Americans. In addition, other brown-skinned citizens of selected Muslim countries were required by the Immigration and Naturalization Services to appear for fingerprinting, photographs, and interrogation under oath.

As my wife previously indicated, this was not a good omen. Nor was the public's failure to protest the arbitrary arrests, without charges and without due process.

The next day, after a restless night, I went to work despite an uneasy feeling in my stomach. I did not know to whom I could turn for protection when a government was putting my liberties at risk. The word "liberty" made me think of the ACLU, the American Civil Liberties Union. I called their local office and talked to Robert Sutherland from the Central Illinois Chapter. He directed me to their branch office in Chicago, and I got hold of an assistant counselor to whom I told my story. He promised to help me.

He called back in the afternoon with plenty of information, and offered to have one of their lawyers represent me, except that I had to wait until the lawyer traveled to Central Illinois. When I indicated that I was eager to quickly bring my FBI problem to a close, he advised me to meet with them only in the presence of a lawyer and to take notes during the interview.

That evening, after our children went to sleep, my wife and I sat down at the kitchen table to discuss the FBI matter. Having never been in trouble with the law, we realized we did not have a lawyer. My wife suggested that maybe her boss, a long time resident of Bloomington, could refer us to one. We called him that night and got a name. Yet, my wife still looked worried.

"We are not in Algeria any longer!" I said, "We are here in America where laws protect people from government abuses. And with a lawyer at my side, I do not think we should worry."

"Why is the government then going only after terrorist suspects and never after suspects of hate crimes? I have not heard of the FBI arresting one single suspect of a hate crime. Are they trying to prevent hate crimes? Or will they show up after a crime has been committed?"

"They cannot arrest hate crime suspects," I said.

"And why not?" she asked.

"Maybe the government knows there would be too many of them to arrest," I explained.

"Then keep fooling yourself about having rights in America, if you want," she added.

"Even if the FBI suspects me of being a terrorist, it is better to be in America than in Algeria," I replied.

"How is that?" she asked, puzzled.

"Here, at least I can buy garbanzo beans at any time of the day and night," I said, thinking she would laugh.

"You might do that only if you don't get arrested and detained without trial or access to a lawyer like all the others suspects," she pointed out.

"But I am not an Arab. I am a Berber, and I don't go to the mosque," I replied.

"Look! Remember what happened to Balbir Singh Sodhi, the Sikh faith follower from India?" she asked.

"Yes," I said, vaguely recollecting his reported murder somewhere in Arizona.

"He was murdered because his killer thought he was either Arab or Muslim. Do you think that people who cannot tell an Arab from a Sikh could tell an Arab from a Berber?" she asked.

I did not answer. She had a point. Two other related killings occurred on September 15. A 48-year old Egyptian Christian Copt and father of three was killed in front of his import shop in Los Angeles. A Pakistani storeowner was found shot to death outside his grocery store in Dallas.

"I don't understand you. The FBI is after you and you behave like an excited little bird. I have been telling you that these are not the times to get out your photography gear and take pictures of railroad tracks. But you refuse to listen to me and you even get mad at me for trying to tell you to be careful," she continued.

I said nothing.

"I am tired of hearing about your hobby. Listen to me. A hobby that can destroy you is nothing but fire. I worry but I am powerless when I see you play with fire when I....also...might get burned," she said as she turned around and in a hurry went back upstairs.

I remained silent as I remembered the many times we had arguments when I would stop to take pictures during our road trips after the 9/11 events. Despite my wife's relentless objections and warnings, I refused her advice to lay low because of my brown skin. Although she would remind me that the times were not for pictures, I still got out of the car to take pictures of scenes and subjects that had attracted my eyes. One day, she even said that I had somewhat changed since I had become a US citizen.

Although my first impulse was to deny such a change, I started to mull it over. Changing my status from foreign student status to US citizen had been a long and bureaucratic process. Once I became a citizen, I felt that I had gained the highest citizenship possible on this rotating planet. However, I wondered if a feeling of arrogance had not crept into my mind along with the pride in my university diplomas and citizenship certificate. In exchange, I must have unfortunately lost some of my modesty and humility during this process.

Then I realized what a major *faux pas* I had made about being Berber, as opposed to Arab. A large majority of Arabs, whether they attend prayers in mosques or not, have nothing to do with terrorism. Why should they be profiled and not me? I thought about Sam, an Arab Muslim friend from Jordan, who worked for a Fortune 500 company's IT department. When the father of his American colleague, John, had gotten sick, Sam covered John's shift at the help desk for a week while he tended to his father's needs. Upon his return, John offered to treat Sam to lunch as a thank you gesture. Sam refused to accept and said to him:

"It was my treat to you for taking care of your father. Not too many people take time to help their elderly parents these days."

Later, I learned that the FBI agents in Sam's town interrogated him too. They had called him at home and asked to meet him at his home. When he refused, they threatened to show up at his work. To avoid being humiliated in front of his co-workers, Sam chose to live the moments of shame and interrogation in the privacy of his home. When I attempted to get him to talk about the interrogation by the FBI, he refused.

I would like to believe in M.L. King Jr.'s dream in which people would not be judged by the color of their skin but by the content of their character. But, after all this categorizing of people based on what they appear instead of what they do reminded me of George Gurdjieff's story about the magician and the sheep. There was a magician whose thousands of sheep were afraid of him and hid in the forest. They had run away because he killed one sheep a day. By telling them different stories about who exactly they were, the magician succeeded in convincing them to come back home and never to run away again. Yet, they still saw sheep being killed and butchered every day, and none of them thought it was his concern because one sheep had been told he was a lion, another a tiger, another a man. Upon returning from the fields, nobody was a sheep except the one who would be slaughtered that day.

On Friday, January 24, as we drove downtown Bloomington to meet our lawyer, my wife confided that, while driving to and from work, she had kept looking in the rear-view mirror to check if the FBI was following her.

"Don't be so paranoid," I said as I wondered whether they had followed me around, too.

"Don't you think a general paranoia is taking over the country and fear is being spread among citizens?" she asked.

"It's a good tool of control and manipulation," I replied.

After we arrived at the lawyer's office, the secretary introduced us to the lawyer and his assistant, who led us into a conference room. My wife sat to my left, and the two lawyers sat across the table from us. After we broke the ice by talking about life's generalities, I recounted my encounter with the state trooper and the call from the FBI and showed them my published work. Probably sensing the sadness in my voice, the lawyer indicated that profiling, such as that of the white people who change sidewalks when they see a black man walking in front or behind them, was a fact of life.

"It is quite different when it is the government, which is supposed to protect you, that starts profiling you," I indicated.

When I finished telling my story, the lawyer indicated that I did not have to meet with the FBI, though he sug-

Sea Port of Bejaia in 1986. The offices of the Algerian National Bank were behind me.

Fatima, my 19-year-old sister-in-law. Two days before she was killed by a car bomb in Algiers, she told her math teacher that she dreamt she was a bride wearing a white dress. When she left to school on May 6, 1997, her mother followed her into the street, as if she sensed it was the last time she would ever see her daughter alive.

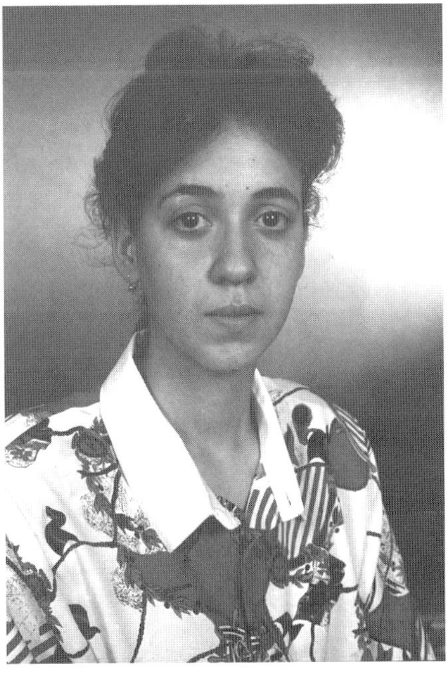

Spiders in a world of their own.

Perseverance in reconstruction.

Shed stories on Route 66.

A row of corn elevators.

Rail tracks and obsolete telephones poles along Route 66. The picture also shows the Illinois State trooper car, traveling north with its headlights turned on .

July 12, 2001: Demonstration against the Algerian President's visit to the White House.

July 12, 2001: Demonstration against the Algerian President's visit to the White House.

Ultimate Band List Decal on my notepad.

Khalil Bendib

gested that I go ahead with the interview just to get them off my back. He added that I did not have to show them any of my published work.

The lawyer's confidence suddenly made the idea of meeting the FBI look more attractive, if still scary. I did not want to miss the opportunity, and I was eager to know exactly what else the FBI wanted to know about me because they already had my fingerprints and other documentation from 1997 when I applied for citizenship. I agreed to his fees and gave him the green light to represent me and to set up an appointment with the FBI.

The following Monday, my lawyer called to tell me that he had talked to the FBI agent in charge of the follow-up. The interview was to take place at the FBI office on Friday, January 31, 2003 at 9:00 a.m.

6

Floating at the Top of the Melting Pot

> It took us almost 100 years to get rid of slavery right here in the Land of the Free, it took us another 100 years to get rid of legal discrimination based on race and gender…
>
> **Molly Ivins**

On the morning of the interview, I met my lawyer outside the FBI offices on Susan Drive in Normal just behind Wal-Mart. Once in the hallway, an agent ushered us to an office with four chairs, a small office desk, a PC hooked up to the Internet, a metallic bookshelf filled with plastic binders, and a black and white picture of J. Edgar Hoover above it. There was a second door behind the desk which connected to the other offices.

Seeing the agent bolt the entrance door behind us, I wondered whether he would let me leave after the interview. He came around the desk, introduced himself as Robert H. and showed both my lawyer and me his FBI badge. Until then I had only seen that metallic government seal on TV and have consequently learned to be unconsciously intimidated by its image. The sight of the real FBI insignia made me uneasy because it had just empowered him. Before the interview started, he and I were already on unequal footing. He indicated that he was the one who had talked to me on the phone and invited us to sit down.

The second door soon opened, and a person, probably Agent Robert's supervisor, came in and introduced himself as Mike E. He began to explain the situation and indicated that the FBI gets information from various sources, from both other law enforcement agencies and concerned citizens—some of it credible, some of it not. Their job was to collect the information and then decide what to do about it. The particular incident involving me, he explained to us, was reported as "an observation of an unusual activity with the detained man [me] taking pictures too low and too close to the railroad tracks." I wanted to interrupt and say that getting closer to the subject is the universal advice in photography, but I refrained. He then finished by saying that all they wanted was my version of the incident.

I looked at my lawyer for a sign to start to tell my side of the story. Instead of giving me the go-ahead, he asked the agent on what basis they thought the reported activity was suspicious.

"Was it the physical appearance or the kneeling down to take pictures? Was it a case of profiling?" my lawyer asked.

Agent Mike summarized for us the state trooper's report, without indicating the reasons for suspicion. When I pointed out that the employer information was incorrect and that my employer was not State Farm Insurance, the agent suggested that the state trooper most likely did not remember my employer's name. I, on the other hand, believed that the trooper must have thought I was one of the Indians who work for State Farm Insurance in Bloomington. In hindsight, I thought it more likely that whether I was from India or Algeria and working for one American company or another made no difference to the trooper and that a foreigner's accent and complexion probably amounted to enough evidence for suspicion.

I took a peek at the letter on the agent's desk and learned that a report had been forwarded by the Illinois State Police to the Amtrak police, an arm of the federal government, before it made the rounds of the FBI offices in Dallas and Chicago, to finally end up in Normal. To realize that my name was the subject of such law enforcement process surprised me a great deal.

The discussion then turned to the rights and wrongs of profiling, with the FBI agent telling a few stories. In one case, the lead was about a group of Middle Easterners who had used the same credit card to pay for a scuba diving trip in Florida. The suspects were called in and proved that the trip had been their annual get-together. Their use of one credit card merely simplified the reservation process. My lawyer then told us of his German ancestors who were shunned and profiled during WW I.

Instead of convincing me to accept racial profiling because it happened to other people, these two stories became two additional reasons to condemn it. That is why, when Agent Mike asked if I understood the FBI's work, I indicated that I understood that they said they were trying to catch terrorists, but that I did not understand their suspecting me. He admitted that although this did indeed seem like a case of profiling, they could not overlook any possible terrorist activity.

My lawyer interrupted: "If my client were Swedish-looking, nothing would have happened? Was it a case of profiling?"

"Sure," Agent Mike agreed without hesitation.

His explicit response shocked me. I could not believe my ears. His response proved that this whole incident was a government's blatant violation of the U.S Constitution, which is supposed to protect people from discrimination based on race and national origin. Not only did it trample the Constitution, it was a human rights violation too and amounted to a collective punishment for people with my complexion.

I understood that I was defenseless and that nothing could protect me from government abuse. My lawyer had just witnessed the trampling of the American Constitution and he did not object. That meant one thing: The interview had to take place. There was no alternative.

Could Agent Mike's response and use of the "sure" be an error, resulting from his having too much power? The intonation in his voice lacked the irony one hears when "sure" is preceded by "yeah." His tone carried neither indifference nor caution; instead, it embodied confidence and certainty, beyond any doubt.

I was surprised not only by the agent's succinct answer but also by my lawyer's failure to object to the unconstitutional discrimination. Both the XIV Amendment of the U.S. Constitution and the U.S. Civil Rights Act of 1866 and 1960 forbid discrimination and ethnic profiling. That left me wondering whether the FBI agent could claim to ignore the laws or to have been ordered by his supervisor to trample citizens' rights. I wondered whether the U.S. Constitution amounted to nothing but beautiful, yet powerless, handwriting on an old and large piece of paper.

Then I started to think that I was in the wrong too: I was guilty of having believed in the powers of the Constitution. I should not have believed that the more than two-century-old ink scribbling, imprisoned in a piece of paper, could protect me from the abuses by other humans, for it was not made of steel. Like my wife, I should have been more skeptical of official claims and rhetoric. But it was too late, and I watched helplessly as my belief in the Constitution crumbled. Yet I still wished its words to come alive, jump off the original paper, and fly to Central Illinois to my rescue.

"Well, maybe the U.S. Constitution has been suspended?" I thought to myself. Because I could not have missed such big news, only one theory could explain why a federal government agent would violate the Constitution I thought was still in effect: It had secretly been suspended.

In the same thread, could it be that the words "human rights, democracy, freedom, justice, equality, land of opportunity, liberty, melting pot, checks and balances, support for the troops, fairness and balance, country, homeland, way of life" were devoid of any meaning? With time, these words seemed magically to have created the adult's equivalent of a children's fairy tale in my mind. The ideas interwoven in them might have obscured my assessment of reality to the point that I had become a domesticated, mindless creature. I seemed to have been manipulated by the daily news headlines that echoed officials lines as if these were divine truths.

Despite a total of 18 years as a law-abiding citizen in this country and despite my educational and professional accomplishments, I was surprised to find out that I was no longer submerged in American life and culture. Instead, I found myself floating at the top of the melting pot called America, sticking out as a target for ethnic profiling and random racist violent crime.

7

Third Still Moment

If tyranny and oppression come to this land, it will be in the guise of fighting a foreign enemy.

James Madison
U.S. President (1809-1817)

Agent Mike asked Agent Robert if he was ready to start the interview, then turned around and left through the second door. Before the interview started, my lawyer and the agent struck up a discussion that soon diverted to football, and Agent Robert confessed to being a fan of the Hoosiers, the University of Indiana football team. Although football conversations usually have a soporific effect on me, spectator sports seemed, without any doubt, to be a safer hobby than photography and a safer haven for conversation.

When the formal interview began, the first questions focused on information I knew the FBI already had: Name and address. Then the agent asked me for my parents' names, parents' residence, my workplace, title and supervisor's name (sorry Dave), date of employment, school and relatives in the U.S., and my wife's name. Like a surgeon's scalpel, the intrusive questions poked me, each cutting deeper and deeper, and the dissection, though physically painless, was mentally traumatizing. I regretted having agreed to the interview, for while I had done nothing wrong, I had to divulge both personal and professional information to prove my innocence. I felt as if some powerful system had negated the principle "innocent until proven guilty," or that it somehow did not apply to me.

I had a feeling of *déjà vu*: I saw the Algerian policeman at the police station in 1986. The agent's blank face and small but muscular body made him an extension of a repressive system. How interesting to see that repression and love of power easily cross cultural, national, and religious boundaries!

When Agent Robert asked me for my children's names, I did not answer. A deep revulsion prohibiting me from pronouncing their names grew in me. My lips refused to move as I imagined them in some futuristic, know-it-all oppressive KGB-style Homeland Security Department files: "Algerian-born father took pictures of railroad tracks. Suspected by Police. Questioned by the FBI. Files distributed to…"

To pronounce their names would be to sully their beautiful innocence and their young lives. I did not want them to be mentioned in the files the FBI has on me. Instead I wanted to scream, "I just love photography. Stop dissecting me like a laboratory animal!" But even the words "You cannot do this to me" stayed inside my mind.

The presence of my lawyer comforted me. He knew the law and could step in—at least I hoped he would—in case the FBI tried to force their names out of me.

Wanting my children's names! Or was that some psychological procedure to get me to feel comfortable with simple questions and to catch me off guard with the serious ones?

The agent did not object to my refusal, and he asked me to recount the incident off Route 66. I started by telling them about my freelance work, and that a simple search of my name on the Internet would have revealed most of my work.

"Is your name common?" he asked.

"No, I am probably the only person in the world with such a name," I said. Right there he got on the Internet and performed a search, which brought up several links.

"I'll look at them later," he said. I wondered whether the FBI had already researched me. After all, they asked me other questions for which they already had answers.

When I glanced again at the agent's notebook, I noticed we were getting to the last couple of questions, saved as the dessert course, but not a sweet one as I was to find out.

"Do you know anyone, associates or friends, who may be working for any terrorist government or terrorist organization?" he asked.

"Personally or by reading newspapers?" I inquired with a touch of wit.

"Personally," he confirmed after a short pause.

I looked at him straight in the eyes and answered:

"No."

"Are you a terrorist or linked to a terrorist organization?" he asked.

For a second, the question appeared easy to answer because it was very obvious to me, and I hoped my lawyer would intervene. His remaining silent meant I had no alternative but to answer it. He had already failed to object to the ethnic profiling when Agent Mike trampled on the Constitution. I also remembered his advice that the only way to get the FBI off my back was to meet with them. I realized then that this was neither an interview nor a meeting; this was an interrogation! Why were there no alternatives to this ordeal for me?

Then the question became hard to answer. As its ten words settled in my mind and I started to examine it, time suddenly froze, creating a third still moment. Nothing moved; neither did I. So, I screamed in complete silence, hoping that my wife's warm and soft hand would touch me and wake me up from the nightmare. My mind was again withdrawing from reality. I almost got dizzy as if I had received a blow on the head. Completely disconnected from my world, I blacked out as if a fast train had unexpectedly dropped me off at a station in a ghost town. Disallowed and discarded, I watched the cars pass by, fast enough so that I could not get back in, but slow enough to see the life inside.

When the train started to slow down, I thought my ordeal was over with and jumped in the door that had just opened. Yet, before I could gather my thoughts and ready myself for new circumstances, I found myself inside the same FBI office, sitting in a chair. I readied myself when I recognized both the FBI agent and the lawyer behind their masks. Across from me, the agent represented an extrapolation of a mean and dangerous machine. To my right, the lawyer resembled the machine's auxiliary piece of equipment, useful but not completely required. Both were waiting for my answer.

I was tempted to laugh so heartily that I would fall from the chair. Me? A terrorist? Could the agent be joking? No, this was serious business. He was not joking, and a laugh might trigger his anger. My desire to laugh consequently morphed into feelings of resentment, sadness, and bitterness, which suddenly gathered in one camp in my mind. Outside, my school diplomas, my professional career, and my citizenship certificate stood, wondering about their usefulness and worth.

To free my imprisoned emotion, I needed to rebel and throw up my learned docility and risk my corruptive privileges. An idea crossed my mind —yes, I thought about getting up and walking out of the FBI office, ending therefore the interrogation, which was only my lawyer's suggestion after all. But, I remained seated. I needed to break down the walls of my acquired self-censorship and discipline and to help my heart voice its pain. However, a feeling of powerlessness mixed with a societal cowardice stopped me short of hastily speaking my mind.

My means to fight against the monstrous machine were limited. To appear disloyal or unpatriotic in front of the FBI agent would be detrimental. I was too close to the monster, and I could feel the heat in its belly. I refrained from uttering the slightest objection to the homeland security policy of ethnic profiling, whose pattern resembled that of a once thought by-gone era.

Nothing seemed obvious to me anymore, and I did not need to run any additional risk. The door to the combustion chamber could suddenly open and the agent with the short haircut could drag me inside to be burned by an endless repressive process that would destroy me and my family.

I had not answered the question that shamed, degraded, and humiliated me into complete silence. I thought that being asked whether I was a terrorist was the worst accusation and insult ever hurled at me. I felt ashamed, because if people saw a terrorist in me, then there must be something wrong with me. I felt degraded, because despite my accomplishments in life they still saw me as a terrorist. I felt humiliated because my humanity was not recognized. How could I be a terrorist? Where is the state of mind of the terrorist in me? Where is the anger that would blind my eyes from seeing the suffering of others? Where are the political propaganda and the religious arguments that would have made me a violent person? Where is the illogical reasoning in me that would justify violent acts against people I know or do not know?

Deep inside me, I knew that my color and my accent were not at fault. I knew better and I know better. Both were real assets. That I have an accent does not indicate any imperfection. It simply means that I spoke three completely different languages for 18 years before I even learned English. That my color is brown does not mean that I am a violent person or a follower of Usama Bin Laden. It only means that I do not have to go to the beach or a tanning salon for a tan. Moreover, like many things in life, terrorists come in different colors, shapes, attitudes, and disguises.

What I deeply believe is that the shame and humiliation should be reserved for those who issue laws to profile others, those who blindly apply them, and finally those who allow such laws to be passed. Yet, the worst shame should be on those who spread and promote such racist ideas through media and government policies and then turn around to profit from them, either through remunerations, product sales, or service contracts.

I hoped my lawyer would intervene and state that I had nothing to do with terrorism. When he remained silent, I knew that I had to answer the question. No one else could come to my rescue. Across from me, Agent Robert remained calm, totally indifferent to his question, perhaps unaware of its profound impact on me.

At the FBI office, caught between the crushing wheels of a mob psychology powered by a subservient hierarchy, I was defenseless, without logic, and almost without humanity. The question had disoriented me and its echoes continued to resonate in my mind. Without any warning, it had destroyed my identity. The pain in my heart grew, and a knot formed in my throat, but my eyes remained dry at all times. It was not time for tears and I needed to steel myself against any terrible ordeal that might lie ahead. My salvation required that I control my anger and pain and show my strength.

I looked Agent Robert straight in the eye.

"No," I answered again, but this time with determination in my voice. It was as if something was helping me pronounce the word to save what remained of my pride as a human being.

After I had answered the question, time restarted. Either sensing my revulsion or switching to the good-cop role, Agent Robert pointed out that the government was just trying to do things the best way it could. His words sounded familiar. They were just like those of the Algerian policeman who, in 1986, recited to me the government's reasons for having to limit my freedoms. Worried that I might anger the federal agent, I refrained from protesting against the FBI policies of ethnic profiling and telling him that he was an accessory to a repressive system. All I wanted was to get out of that office, be with my family, and take more pictures of railroad tracks, telephone poles, and spider webs.

8

Marrying the Devil

> Do not condemn us, you above all. We have educated you. We have given you a formidable weapon. We want your gratitude. Of course we are not asking you to compromise yourself—you are a family man. All we ask is that you plug your ears and close your eyes, nothing more.
>
> **Mouloud Feraoun**
>
> *Journal 1954-1962: Reflections on the French-Algerian War*

My lawyer belatedly intervened to indicate to the agent that he had seen my pictures and my writings and could confirm that my interest in photography was purely artistic.

The agent then asked if I had a request, wanted to share a concern or whether anyone had threatened or bothered me. I thought to answer with irony and tell him that indeed an organization called the FBI had bothered me. Realizing that he would probably find my answer inappropriate, I did not say anything. I practiced self-censorship again.

But I could not miss the golden opportunity to share at least one concern. It was the Bush Administration's support of the military dictatorship in Algeria and its supplying of arms to it. Not only did the Bush Administration choose to turn a blind eye to the Algerian government's continued repression and human rights violations, but it also strengthened its ties to it.

The relations between the U.S. and Algeria reached a climax when President Bush hosted President Abdelaziz Bouteflika on July 12, 2001 at the White House. Outside, more than 200 people, mostly from Algeria, gathered to denounce the meeting of the two presidents and to protest the massive repression that was taking place in the Berber region of Kabylia. One sign the demonstrators held called for trying Bouteflika and the military junta at the International Tribunal in The Hague for crimes against humanity.

That the meeting of Bush and Bouteflika at the White House turned out to be a business deal was no surprise at all. Indeed, a few months after that meeting, Algeria awarded a $700 million energy contract to Kellog-Brown-Root (KBR), a Halliburton subsidiary. As reported by *The Los Angeles Times* of July 12, 2001 issue, Haliburton's operations in Algeria were more profitable during Dick Cheney's 1995-1999 tenure as its CEO. During that period, the current vice-president traveled to Algeria and met twice with President Bouteflika. In 2000 KBR received half of the $267.7 million in loans and guarantees issued by the Import-Export Bank, a federal institution financed with taxpayers' money, for projects in Algeria.

But outside the White House, my friends' voices and mine did not influence President Bush's agenda a bit. His administration's claim to value freedom, democracy, and human rights appeared be a scratch-thin superficial veneer. Walking the talk was not Bush's forte. Furthermore, his rhetorical claims were only mesmerizing catchwords relayed by willing news organizations for national consumption. "Marrying the devil or at least sleeping with him" seemed to fit the Bush Administration's relation with most of the North African and Middle Eastern countries. Once more, money was louder, and it prevailed over human rights and justice.

A few weeks before the meeting of the two presidents, while the Berbers in Kabylia were being massacred in broad daylight by Algerian paramilitary forces, a friend living in Washington D.C managed to meet with the Algeria Desk officer at the State Department. My friend expressed his surprise at the Bush Administration's silence after more than 100 Berber protesters were killed and more than 3,000 others were injured. By contrasting the virulent condemnations of the Tiananmen Square events in China by the first Bush Administration with the total silence of the current Bush Administration vis-à-vis the Kabylia events, my friend sought to point out to the officer that perhaps there was a double standard in US foreign policy.

The desk officer was shocked that my friend had dared to question the actions of the US Government. He then bluntly stated that Algeria was no comparison to China and explained that unlike China, the US had no interest in Algeria. The officer's response left my friend completely disillusioned with the claims America makes about defending freedom and democracy in the world.

The Desk Officer explained further to my friend that when it came to treatment of minorities, only Congress could affect US foreign policy towards Algeria. Such an endeavor would require the creation of a lobby with lots of money to which neither my friend nor I had access. We were out of luck. Instead, we and a few other mutual friends poured our hearts into a four-page-long letter that detailed Algeria's undemocratic institutions, its human rights violations, and repressive policies. It became an open letter addressed to the US Ambassador to Algeria on May 20, 2002.

Only much later—after reading several of Noam Chomsky's books and listening to Amy Goodman's DemocracyNow program—that my friend and I finally understood what the Algeria Desk Officer was talking about, though we still are not sure the officer himself was actually aware of the true meaning of his own statements. During the 1989 Tiananmen Square incident in China, an independent country, the US did not miss the opportunity to make the Chinese government unpopular at home and abroad by condemning its actions. However, when much more serious human rights violations take place in Algeria, now a vassal state, it never utters any criticism.

The Bush Administration's priorities in Algeria are unfortunately deals and profits, and energy contracts and arms sales are enough to buy Washington's silence on Algeria's human rights abuses. Indeed, several State Department officials went as far as praising Algeria for its fight against terrorism and issuing laughable statements on Algeria's progress towards greater democracy. Unfortunately, the more than 200,000 civilian victims and the 10,000 disappearances cannot testify to Algeria's excellent protection of its poor and powerless citizens.

Two other events in two different countries, Algeria and Iran, illustrate another case of double standards in US foreign policy. The first event took place on June 14, 2001 when more than a million Berbers marched in Algiers to protest the killing of unarmed civilians in Kabylia. Government forces intervened, and more than 10 people died. Both President Bush and the White House spokesman, Ari Fleisher, said nothing.

The second event took place on June 14, 2003 in Teheran when thousands of Iranians organized a protest. Government forces intervened. A few injuries were reported but not one death. President Bush declared: "This is the beginnings of people expressing themselves toward a free Iran which I think is positive." Ari Fleischer added: "The United States views with great concern the use of violence against Iranian students peacefully expressing their political views."

The US silence on the Algerian government's disrespect of human rights can be summarized by the statements of one retired State Department diplomat. A former US Ambassador to Algeria, who met a friend at a conference, openly uttered criticism of Bouteflika, who had just been elected. When my friend inquired why he kept quiet when he was at his post in Algiers, the former Ambassador replied: "At that time, I was paid to be a diplomat and not to criticize the host government."

In 2002, Algeria organized both municipal and legislative elections, and the Kabylia region decided to boycott them because the government's repression the year before left the people more distrustful of the authorities than ever. The Algerian government, despite being a dictatorship, needed to window-dress itself as a democracy, and therefore needed to hold elections. That was when the State Department stepped in and got involved in Algerian internal politics. Five officials at the US Embassy in Algiers traveled to Kabylia twice to avert the Berber boycott. However, the Berber political grassroots leaders held onto their position and refused to participate. They knew that the elections were rigged from the start, since they were staged by the same government officials that gave orders to shoot civilians with live bullets a year earlier.

"If you are not going to vote, do you plan to take power by force?" one envoy asked ominously.

In return, the grassroots leaders took this opportunity to ask the Embassy officials the reasons they did not show up when the Algerian paramilitary forces were shooting at unarmed protesters.

"We could not then," answered the envoy.

Kabylia did not vote, and the US State Department did not hail Algeria as a democratic country.

Washington's silence is matched by that of the mainstream news media. When they report on Algeria, their news accounts completely distort the issues at hands. One *New York Times* report, dated June 18, 2001, had the following headline, "Berber Unrest Threatens Algeria's Government," but failed to mention that the 2001 street protest erupted after an 18-year Berber student died at the hands of the paramilitary police. Such headlines twisted the issue completely and failed to show how the government was a threat to the Berbers in particular and the Algerian people in general, and not the other way around.

The December 20, 2001 issue of the same newspaper reported on "Berber Anger." The reporter purposely failed to indicate that Berbers have a problem with the Algerian government whose policies are discriminatory and violent. Instead, the article spun the political problem into an ethnic one, stating that Berbers accused the Arabs of oppression. Fortunately, it is easy to realize that the problem in Algeria is not ethnic because many high civilian and military officials are Berbers. Still another article, published by *The New York Times* on December 9, 2002, justified the sale of arms to Algeria but said nothing about the imprisonment of the leaders of the Berber grassroots movement.

Ironically, 21 years earlier, when Algeria faced its first popular protest since its independence and in the same region, it accused both the US and France of being behind it: The headline of the April 25, 1980 issue of *The New York Times* read "Algeria Accuses US and others in Berbers' Unrest." Although the Algerian government still claimed that the 2001 protests were the work of foreign agents, it mentioned neither France nor the US, because both Bush and Chirac had become friends with Bouteflika and the generals.

Other media outlets such as NPR News (known in some circles as National Propaganda Radio or National Petroleum Radio and sometimes called the FOX News with Cappuccino for the intellectuals) mostly defend the sale of arms to the Algerian military. When they report on Algeria, they usually do so with silk gloves and they sidestep all of the Algerian political problems and issues.

Both *The New York Times* and NPR News failed to report on the imprisonment of journalists such as Benchicou and cartoonist Ali Dilem. Neither issued a report on the State of Emergency Law, in effect since 1992, or on Algeria's restrictive 2001 penal code amendments that undermines constitutional provisions for freedom of speech. When Abassi Madani and Ali Belhadj, two spiritual and political leaders of the FIS party, were released from jail in July 2003, Algerian authorities banned foreign media from covering the event. Two French TV news crews were expelled for ignoring the ban. On this side of the Atlantic Ocean, both *The New York Times* and NPR News failed to report on the event. Such is the mainstream media's treatment of news about a country that is a US client state.

9

My Link to UBL

> We must not let our patriotic conviction make outlaws of us, paradox of paradoxes. For, as all of you know, the law has never defended just causes—in fact, it has nothing to do with justice or truth.
>
> **Tahar Djaout**
> *The Watchers*

I realized that I did not have much time to share my concern with the FBI agent. If I openly criticized Bush's foreign policies, I imagined hearing the federal agent say "You don't like America" and "You hate our freedom." Such responses were reminiscent of the "You don't believe in God" or "You are against Islam," some of my co-workers in the Sahara used to say back in the 1980s whenever I disagreed with their political arguments for an Islamic state in Algeria.

The polarized political atmosphere throughout America has created a virtually binary world of "us" and "them." A criticism from my side would automatically put me in the second group, making me an unwilling proponent of the "them" group. That would be more trouble for me, for I was already too close to the monstrous machine.

Fearing to appear disloyal or unpatriotic, I decided to censor myself once more. What would I gain if I dissented, uttered my opposition or showed my skepticism at President Bush's foreign or domestic policies?

Instead, I asked the agent almost laughingly whether he could put pressure on the Algerian government to stop its repressive policies.

He remained silent, like a stone, not a sound or a change in his facial expression. Only his eyes blinked.

"Can I get a government card from you saying that I am allowed to take pictures?" I said jokingly, to loosen up the atmosphere and switch to a less political issue.

He did not smile, but suggested that I call my lawyer if I get stopped again for taking pictures. I understood then that ethnic profiling had no end in sight.

The interview was over as far as he was concerned. I closed my notepad, which I used to take notes throughout the interview.

"What is that?" he asked pointing at my notebook.

"That is a notepad," I replied as I displayed it to him.

"No, on the front cover. What does the decal say?"

"Oh, this?" I asked, displaying the cover decal.

"Yes," he said.

The notebook had a circular, silvery plastic decal with a yellow ring. I told him that the letters "UBL," written in the center of the decal, stood for "Ultimate Band List," a music e-store.

"OK," he said after hearing my explanation.

He indicated that we were done with the interview, and the three of us got up. Agent Robert opened the door, and let my lawyer and me into the hall.

"I might write an article about this interview," I told him.

He said that I could but that I should not use his name or that of his supervisor. My lawyer agreed, "Don't use their real names."

"I see that you have the picture of U- B- L here," my lawyer noted to Agent Robert standing near the office door.

On a board to our right, several pictures of people wanted by the FBI were displayed. The one at the top was that of the most wanted man: Usama Bin Laden.

"Yes," Agent Robert answered.

I froze for a second when I realized that my lawyer had just pronounced the same initials as those of the Ultimate Band List e-store and that the FBI agent might have seen a connection between Usama Bin Laden and me because the UBL initials on my notepad matched those of the reported mastermind of the 9/11 attacks.

I turned around towards the agent who was still holding the door behind us.

"Was that the reason you asked me about the UBL letters on my notepad?" I asked, with a smile.

"Yes," he answered.

I was stunned when I realized how naive I was. Both my lawyer and the agent had made the link between my UBL decal and Usama Bin Laden. My lawyer used the initials UBL as if he purposely wanted to expose my naiveté to me.

After my lawyer and I left the FBI office, we said goodbye to one another. I got into my car, and I checked my watch. The time was just past 10:00 am. The interview had only taken an hour, but it had seemed like an eternity. I thought about how life is filled with a series of coincidences: some wonderful, others terrible, still others mind-blowing.

I left the FBI parking lot, turned right on Susan Drive and then right again on Fort Jesse. I thought about heading North to get my kicks on Route 66 one more time. Instead, I drove home.

BIBLIOGRAPHY

"Algeria Accuses US., and others in Berbers' Unrest," *The New York Times*, April 25, 1980, Sec. A, p. 6.

Waldman, Peter , "Algerians Wonder Who's Really Behind Recent Series of High-Profile Murders," *The Wall Street Journal*, July 1, 1993, Sec. A, p. 8, col. 1.

Yous, Nesroulah and Mellah, Salima, *Qui a tué à Bentalha? Chronique d'un Massacre Annoncé*, La Découverte, 2000.

Souaïdia, Habib, *La Sale Guerre*, La Découverte, Paris, 2001.

Daley, Suzanne, "Challenge for Algeria: Berber Anger," *The New York Times*, December 20, 2001, Sec. A, p. 8, col. 3.

Aboud, Hichem, *La Maffia des Généraux*, Lattès, Paris, 2002.

Amazigh –American Committee in Solidarity with Kabylia, "Open Letter to the US Ambassador to Algeria," September 29, 2002, <http://www.kabyle.com/article.php3?id_article=1996> or <http://www.geocities.com/zighenaym/letterUSambassador.html>, (January 23, 2005).

Weisman, Steve. "US to Sell Weapons to Algeria to Help Fight Islamic Radicals," *The New York Times,* December 10, 2002, Sec. A, p. 20, col. 3.

"Berbers in Algeria Refuse Peace Talks ," *The New York Times*, June 30, 2003, Sec. A, p. 9, col. 1.

Le Sueur, James, "Introduction," in Mouloud Feraoun, *The Poor Man's Son*, University of Virginia Press, Charlottesville, 2005.